100

REFLECTIONS

TO MASTER YOUR

MIND

Also by Juan Garcia

Books

100 Reflections

To Heal Your Mind And Soul

The Life You Crave Is Waiting

30 Days to Unlock Confidence, Discipline and the Life You Crave

Website

https://linktr.ee/ibelieveinmegospel

100 Reflections to Master Your Mind

By Juan Garcia

I Believe in Me Gospel Series

First Edition, 2025

ISBN: 979-8-9930795-2-3

Printed in the United States of America
Published by I Believe in Me Gospel
Cover designed by Juan Garcia

i

To the one who has ever felt weak in the face of their own mind.
To the one who has wrestled with doubt, excuses, and fear.
To the one who has wanted to quit but still longs to rise.

This book is for you.
For the fighter inside you.
For the commander waiting to take control.
For the unshakable self you were always meant to become.

This book is yours — and it is a mirror.
Every reflection inside it was written to remind you: you are stronger than you think, and discipline is your proof.

This is for you.

How to Use This Book

This is not a book to read once and shelve. It is a training ground for your mind. Each reflection is a tool, a weapon, a reminder of the discipline required to master yourself.

1. One at a Time
Read a single reflection slowly. Let it sink in. The power is in repetition, not speed.

2. **Morning or Night**
Begin your day with a reflection to set your mind, or end your day with one to reset and realign.

3. **Apply, Don't Just Read**
Each transcript is a mirror. Ask yourself: Where does this apply? What action will I take?

4. **Carry the Gem**
At the end of each reflection is a gem — one line to anchor your mind. Repeat it. Live it.

5. **Repeat the Cycle**
When you finish, return to the beginning. Mastery comes through repetition.

This book is your battlefield. Each reflection is a weapon. Use them daily until they are no longer words — but your way of life.

Table of Contents

42. I train focus like a muscle.
43. I sharpen wisdom through reflection.
44. I master boredom with discipline.
45. I think strategically, not emotionally.
46. I don't seek easy answers.
47. My thoughts align with my purpose.
48. I remove noise to hear truth.
49. I keep my mind sharp through struggle.
50. I don't react; I respond with clarity.
51. My inner dialogue is disciplined.
52. I own my mind, fully and completely.
53. I do what must be done, not what I feel like.
54. My emotions serve me; they do not control me.
55. Pain is feedback, not a reason to quit.
56. I rise faster than I fall.
57. Every day I train the muscle of discipline.
58. I master the small choices that shape my life.
59. I face discomfort; that is where growth lives.
60. My actions prove my words.
61. I don't need easy; I need progress.
62. Weakness dies in my persistence.
63. I do not wait for motivation — I act without it.
64. I endure what others avoid.
65. Success is built on my habits, not my feelings.
66. I sharpen my mind by mastering my body.
67. I am stronger than my excuses.
68. Failure is my teacher, not my identity.
69. I control what I give my attention to.
70. My word is a contract with myself.
71. I don't seek comfort — I create strength.
72. I am unshaken by setbacks.
73. Discipline is freedom; I practice it daily.
74. My future bows to my daily choices.
75. I am consistent, not perfect.
76. I create order in my mind and my life.
77. I am built to endure storms.
78. I push myself where others stop.
79. I am calm under pressure.
80. I sharpen discipline like a blade.
81. Each rep, each step, builds the man I become.
82. I turn resistance into strength.
83. My past does not excuse my present.
84. I am unbreakable when I refuse to quit.

85. I do not run from fear — I walk through it.
86. I own my choices completely.
87. I outlast the noise of doubt.
88. I am patient with the process.
89. I give effort even when no one is watching.
90. I refuse to lie to myself.
91. My self-control is my power.
92. I rise at once when I fall.
93. I am a servant to my higher self, not my impulses.
94. The harder the road, the stronger I become.
95. I am my own commander.
96. My strength is proven daily.
97. I can do hard things again and again.
98. I stay steady while others break.
99. I out-discipline talent.
100. My success is earned, not given.

Introduction

This book will not make you comfortable.
This book will give you clarity, command, and discipline.

The world will try to master your mind if you don't master
it yourself. Distractions, impulses, fears, and doubts are
always waiting to take control. Most people live as
servants to these forces, drifting through life without
direction. This book exists so you will not be one of them.

100 Reflections to Master Your Mind is not meant to be read
once and forgotten. this is your manual. Your training
ground. Your mirror. Each reflection is a challenge and a
tool — short enough to remember, deep enough to
confront you, and practical enough to shape the way you
live.

Inside, you will not find empty words or easy answers.
You will find truths sharpened to cut through illusion.
You will find reminders that demand action, not excuses.
You will find discipline made real on the page —
discipline that must be practiced daily if you are to
command your life fully.

This book will not change you. *You will change you.*
The reflections are here to guide you, to push you, to
confront you when you drift, and to remind you when you
forget. But in the end, it is your consistency, your
persistence, your discipline that will shape your destiny.

Approach these pages with seriousness. Carry them with
you. Return to them when you stumble, when you feel
weak, when you are tempted to quit. They will not
comfort you — they will call you higher.

It's simple: your mind is not your master. It is your servant. And when you master it, you will unlock the freedom, the strength and the future that was always waiting for you.

This is your book. This is your training ground. This is your command.

The kingdom of heaven is within you.
Luke 17:21

Reflection 1: I am not my thoughts; I choose which to follow.

Not every thought I have is me.

I remind myself daily: my mind creates thousands of thoughts, and most are noise. Some are fears from my past. Some are judgments I inherited. Some are just random sparks. But they're not all me.

When my mind says, *"You can't do this,"* I stop and remember: that's just a thought, not a fact. When it says, *"You always fail,"* I breathe and remind myself: I'm the one who decides what's true.

I am not the prisoner of my thoughts. I am the chooser. I decide which ones to follow and which ones to let go. That's my real power.

Gem of Knowledge

I am not what I think — I am what I choose to believe.

Reflection 2: I question every belief that weakens me.

If it makes me small, I question it.

I look at my beliefs the way I'd look at locks on a door. Some keep me safe. Some keep me trapped. And if a belief weakens me — if it makes me doubt myself, shrink, or quit — then I know it's not mine to keep.

Who planted it? A parent? A teacher? A failure from years ago? I remind myself that beliefs are not facts; they're stories. And I can rewrite the story.

When I hear myself think, *"I'm not ready,"* I stop and ask: *Who told me that? Is it even true?* Every time I question weakness, I give strength more room to grow.

Gem of Knowledge

No belief owns me — I choose what to keep.

2

Reflection 3: I direct my focus; it does not wander.

My focus is mine, not the world's.

I live in a world built to steal my attention. Notifications, headlines, opinions — all of it pulling at me. If I let my focus wander, I know my life will wander with it.

So I remind myself: my focus is like a flashlight. Where I shine it, life expands. If I shine it on distractions, they grow stronger. If I shine it on my vision, my vision grows clearer.

Every time I choose where to put my attention, I take my power back. I'm not here to scatter my energy. I'm here to direct it — to build, to create, to live with intention.

Gem of Knowledge

My focus follows me, not the other way around.

Reflection 4: My mind is my servant, not my master.

My mind works for me — not against me.

I know my mind is brilliant, but I also know it can be a tyrant if I let it run unchecked. It overthinks, it worries, it replays the past. But that's not who I am. That's just what it does.

So I remind myself daily: my mind is my tool. It serves my higher will. It calculates, plans, imagines — but it does not command me. I decide. I direct.

When I put myself above my mind, everything shifts. I use it without being used. I think without being consumed. My mind serves my purpose, not the other way around.

Gem of Knowledge

My mind is my tool, not my ruler.

Reflection 5: I think clearly under pressure.

Pressure doesn't crush me — it sharpens me.

When the heat rises, when everything feels like it's closing in, I remind myself: this is my proving ground. Pressure is not here to break me — it's here to reveal me.

I've seen what happens when people panic. They lose themselves. Their breath shortens, their minds race, and they start to make desperate choices. I will not live like that. I choose clarity.

In the middle of chaos, I take a breath. I step back. I remind myself: *What matters most right now? What is the next step forward?* Not every answer, not every outcome — just the next step. That pause alone is power. That pause is the difference between drowning and rising.

I don't run from pressure anymore. I let it train me. Each time I keep calm when others lose control, I sharpen my ability to think clearly. I become unshakable, steady, strong.

Gem of Knowledge

Pressure is my test — and clarity is my answer.

Reflection 6: I do not feed distractions.

Every distraction I feed is a thief stealing my future.

The world is full of noise. It comes disguised as entertainment, as urgency, as something harmless. But every time I give in to distraction, I weaken myself. I give away energy I could have used to build, to grow, to win.

I remind myself: distractions only survive if I feed them. The endless scrolling, the wasted conversations, the habits that leave me empty — they die the moment I stop giving them my attention. What I starve shrinks. What I feed grows.

My attention is sacred. Every time I say *no* to distraction, I say *yes* to my future. Every moment of focus builds something that distraction could never give me: progress. Confidence. Results.

I don't starve distractions because I hate them. I starve them because I love who I am becoming too much to let them steal my time.

Gem of Knowledge

Starving distractions feeds my destiny.

Reflection 7: Doubt is a shadow, not a command.

Doubt is not my truth — it's just the shadow of my fear.

Every time I aim higher, doubt shows up. It whispers in my mind: *"You're not ready. What if you fail? Who do you think you are?"* I used to mistake those whispers for truth. But now I know better.

Doubt is not a command. It has no authority over me. It is only the shadow that appears because I am moving toward light. The bigger the goal, the bigger the shadow.

I remind myself: shadows cannot touch me. They cannot stop me. They only look real when I stand still. The moment I move forward, they shrink and fade.

Courage doesn't mean I never doubt. Courage means I see the doubt, I hear it, and I move forward anyway. And every step I take weakens the shadow's hold.

Gem of Knowledge

Doubt will follow me, but it will never lead me.

Reflection 8: I separate facts from feelings.

My feelings are real, but they are not always the truth.

Some days I feel unstoppable. Other days I feel broken, small, or behind. Feelings change like the weather. If I let them define my reality, I'll be tossed around like a leaf in the wind.

But facts — facts are solid. Feelings might say, *"I can't handle this,"* but the fact is, I've already survived everything life has thrown at me. Feelings might say, *"I'm not enough,"* but the fact is, I keep rising no matter how many times I fall.

I remind myself: feelings deserve respect, but not obedience. I listen to them, I honor them, but I don't mistake them for commands. I check the facts. And when the facts say I can move forward, I move — no matter how I feel.

This is how I protect myself from being ruled by moods. This is how I live anchored instead of drifting.

Gem of Knowledge

Feelings may shift, but facts keep me grounded.

Reflection 9: My patience sharpens my mind.

Patience isn't weakness — it's strength waiting for the right moment.

The world tells me to rush. Hurry to succeed, hurry to prove myself, hurry to get what I want. But rushing has only ever clouded my vision, made me react without thinking, and left me with regrets.

Patience is my weapon. It gives me clarity. When I wait instead of react, I see more. I notice the patterns. I recognize the opportunities that impatience blinds others to.

Every time I breathe before I respond, every time I hold steady when others are frantic, I sharpen my mind. Patience keeps me from being controlled by urgency, fear, or impulse. It allows me to strike when the moment is right — not just when I feel restless.

Patience is not me doing nothing. Patience is me preparing, growing, and positioning myself for the win.

Gem of Knowledge

Patience is not delay — it is strategy.

9

Reflection 10: I prepare in silence and act with power.

My silence is not weakness — it is preparation.

The world is loud. Everyone is announcing their plans, posting their moves, bragging about what they *say* they'll do. But I don't need that noise. I prepare in silence.

In silence, I sharpen my skills. In silence, I build my strength. In silence, I put in the work that no one sees. And when it's time to act, my results speak for me louder than any words ever could.

Silence is my strategy. Noise doesn't build anything — but discipline in the dark does. And when the right moment comes, I don't have to announce. I don't have to prove. I simply act, and the world feels the power I've been building all along.

Gem of Knowledge

I train in silence so my actions roar.

Reflection 11: I train my mind daily.

If I don't train my mind, it trains me.

I know my mind is like a muscle. If I don't work it, it weakens. If I don't shape it, it shapes me. Every day, thoughts try to run wild — fears, distractions, negativity. And every day, I must show up like a trainer in the gym.

Training my mind isn't just about positivity. It's about discipline. It's about catching the useless thought before it roots. It's about reminding myself of truth when lies try to sneak in. It's about choosing clarity instead of confusion, strength instead of weakness.

I don't wait until life gets hard to start training my mind. I train it daily, so when challenges come, I'm already strong. My mind works for me because I condition it. I lead it. I train it.

Gem of Knowledge

What I train daily becomes who I am under pressure.

11

Reflection 12: I think long-term, not short-term.

Short-term comfort costs me long-term freedom.

Every day I have a choice: do I reach for what feels good right now, or do I invest in what will make me stronger tomorrow? Most people sacrifice their future for their present. I will not.

I remind myself: short-term thinking is a trap. It's why people give up when things get hard. It's why they settle for distractions instead of growth. But I think long-term. I ask: *Where will this decision take me in a year? Five years? Ten?*

When I think long-term, I endure what others can't. I can say *no* to instant pleasure because I see the bigger picture. I can stay patient because I know the reward is coming.

The short-term may tempt me, but the long-term will define me.

Gem of Knowledge

I trade comfort today for strength tomorrow.

Reflection 13: I keep my promises to myself.

The quickest way to destroy trust is to break my own word.

I've learned this: if I can't trust myself, nothing else matters. Every time I say I'll do something and I don't, I chip away at my own confidence. Every broken promise to myself becomes a wound.

But every promise I keep — no matter how small — becomes proof that I can rely on me. Wake up early. Finish the task. Stay disciplined when it's easier to quit. These aren't just habits; they're contracts with myself.

I remind myself: keeping my promises is not about perfection — it's about trust. If I trust myself, I don't need validation from anyone else. I walk stronger because I know my word to myself is law.

Gem of Knowledge

Self-trust is built one kept promise at a time.

Reflection 14: I control my attention like a blade.

My attention cuts through noise like steel.

I live in a world that profits off stealing my focus. Every ad, every distraction, every voice is designed to pull me away from what matters. But I remind myself: my attention is a blade. If I swing it wildly, it's useless. If I sharpen it and direct it, it cuts through anything.

When I focus, I make progress. When I scatter, I lose myself. My attention is my greatest weapon, and I must control it. That means I choose what I look at, what I listen to, what I allow into my mind.

I don't waste the blade on nonsense. I don't dull it with distractions. I keep it sharp, I keep it precise, and I use it to carve my future.

Gem of Knowledge

My attention is a weapon; I wield it with precision.

Reflection 15: I replace complaints with action.

Every complaint is wasted energy that could've built something.

I remind myself: complaining doesn't change anything. All it does is feed the very problem I want to escape. Every word of complaint is me telling myself I'm powerless — and that's a lie I refuse to live in.

When I catch myself complaining, I stop. I breathe. And I ask: *What can I do right now? What step can I take?* Even the smallest action moves me forward. Complaints keep me stuck; action sets me free.

It's easy to talk about what's wrong. Anyone can point out problems. But it takes strength to move past words and into movement. When I replace complaints with action, I become the solution. I take my power back.

I don't waste my breath complaining anymore. I use it to fuel action. I don't talk about change. I live it.

Gem of Knowledge

Complaining drains me. Action transforms me.

15

Reflection 16: I learn from mistakes without self-pity.

A mistake is a lesson, not a life sentence.

I will not waste my mistakes. When I fall short, when I slip, when I get it wrong — I refuse to sit in self-pity. Feeling sorry for myself only doubles the failure.

Instead, I mine mistakes for gold. I ask: *What can I learn here? What truth does this show me? What do I need to do differently next time?* If I get the lesson, the mistake is no longer a weight — it becomes fuel.

Everyone makes mistakes. The difference between the broken and the strong is this: some drown in self-pity, while others rise with wisdom. I choose to rise.

I forgive myself quickly, I learn immediately, and I keep moving forward. Because mistakes don't define me. My response to them does.

Gem of Knowledge

Mistakes don't weaken me; self-pity does.

Reflection 17: I master one thing at a time.

Scattered effort builds nothing. Focused mastery builds everything.

I remind myself: I can do many things in life, but not all at once. If I scatter my effort, I become average at everything and great at nothing. But if I give myself fully to one thing at a time, I build mastery.

Mastery requires patience. It requires discipline. It requires saying *no* to distractions, *no* to shiny new pursuits, and *yes* to repetition, to practice, to refining my craft. That's not weakness — that's strength.

I know the world loves multitasking, but I love results. I'd rather pour myself into one thing and become unshakable than chase ten things and remain fragile. When I master one thing, it gives me confidence to master the next, and the next.

I focus. I choose. I commit. And I master one thing at a time — until I am undeniable.

Gem of Knowledge

Greatness is built by mastering the one in front of me.

17

Reflection 18: I read, I study, I grow.

Knowledge is fuel, and I refuse to starve my mind.

I know this truth: growth is not automatic. If I'm not learning, I'm shrinking. If I'm not studying, I'm stagnating. If I'm not feeding my mind, the world will feed me poison.

So I read. I study. I grow. Not because I want to look smart, but because I refuse to be blind. Knowledge expands my vision. It gives me tools. It gives me choices. Every book, every lesson, every study session — they stack inside me, preparing me for battles I don't even see yet.

I don't waste my time filling my head with noise. I choose what I feed on. I feed on wisdom. I feed on truth. I feed on the kind of knowledge that sharpens me into someone who cannot be easily fooled or broken.

Growth isn't something I wait for — it's something I demand from myself. Every page I read, every truth I study, every lesson I take in — it all becomes part of the weapon I am becoming.

Gem of Knowledge

The more I feed my mind, the more unstoppable I grow.

Reflection 19: I guard my mind against poison.

What I allow into my mind becomes the soil of my life.

I remind myself: everything I consume shapes me. Every word I hear, every show I watch, every conversation I entertain — it all plants seeds in my mind. Some seeds grow strength, clarity, and peace. Others grow fear, anger, and weakness.

That's why I guard my mind like it's sacred ground. I refuse to let poison live in me. Gossip, negativity, toxic people, endless noise — they don't get space here. Because I know once they enter, they don't just sit there. They spread.

Guarding my mind doesn't mean I hide from reality. It means I choose what deserves my attention, what earns my focus, what is worthy of shaping me. If it doesn't align with who I want to become, I shut the door.

Every day, I am either feeding my mind medicine or poison. I choose medicine. I choose words that build me, ideas that stretch me, and truths that free me. My mind is my fortress, and I decide who enters.

Gem of Knowledge

If I don't guard my mind, the world will poison it for me.

Reflection 20: My silence holds power.

Silence is not emptiness — silence is strength contained.

I remind myself: not everything requires my reaction. Not every insult deserves my energy. Not every situation needs my voice. Sometimes, the greatest strength is saying nothing.

Silence protects me. In silence, I observe. In silence, I see what others miss because they're too busy talking. In silence, I gather myself. My silence is not weakness; it is strategy.

People mistake noise for power, but real power moves quietly. It doesn't need validation. It doesn't need to prove. Silence makes my words carry more weight when I finally do speak, because I'm not reacting — I'm choosing.

I don't fear silence anymore. I use it. I let it heal me, guide me, and steady me. My silence intimidates those who thrive on chaos, and it strengthens me when I need clarity.

Gem of Knowledge

My silence is not empty — it is charged with power.

Reflection 21: I don't fear failure; I fear inaction.

Failure doesn't scare me. Doing nothing does.

I remind myself: failure is not final. Failure is proof that I tried. Failure carries lessons, strength, and growth that comfort never gives. I can live with falling short — I cannot live with never stepping forward.

The real danger isn't failure; it's inaction. Doing nothing kills dreams before they can even breathe. Doing nothing leaves me with regret, with *what ifs*, with the pain of never knowing. I'd rather fail a thousand times than sit still once.

So I move. Even when I'm uncertain, I move. Even when I'm afraid, I act. Because action creates momentum, and momentum creates possibility. And every time I move, I remind myself: I am alive, I am trying, I am in the fight.

I do not measure myself by my failures — I measure myself by my willingness to act despite them. Fear of failure has no hold on me. Fear of inaction drives me forward.

Gem of Knowledge

Failure is a lesson; inaction is a death sentence.

23

Reflection 22: I train my mind to stay calm.

Calm is not my default — it's my training.

I remind myself: chaos will come. Pressure will rise. Storms will hit when I least expect them. But I don't wait until the storm arrives to decide who I will be. I train myself now.

Staying calm is not about pretending nothing is wrong. It's about holding steady when everything around me shakes. It's about breathing when fear wants me to choke. It's about slowing down when my thoughts want to race.

Every time I choose calm, I grow stronger. I train it like a muscle. One pause instead of a reaction. One breath instead of an outburst. One clear decision instead of a frantic one. Day by day, I build the habit of calm until it becomes my natural response.

Chaos does not control me. Pressure does not define me. My calm is my power — and I train it daily so no storm can take it from me.

Gem of Knowledge

Calm is not given; it is trained.

Reflection 23: I replace excuses with execution.

Excuses don't move me forward — execution does.

I remind myself: excuses sound smart, but they keep me stuck. I can come up with a hundred reasons why I can't — too tired, too busy, too unprepared. But excuses never built anything. Execution does.

When I hear myself starting to excuse, I catch it. I ask: *Is this moving me forward or holding me back?* And then I choose execution. Even if I don't feel ready. Even if it's messy. Even if it's uncomfortable.

Excuses protect my comfort. Execution builds my future. And I can't have both. So I stop waiting for the perfect time. I stop hiding behind reasons. I move.

Action is the antidote to every excuse. Every step I take proves to me that I don't need the perfect plan. I just need to execute.

Gem of Knowledge

Excuses are noise; execution is proof.

Reflection 24: I stay present in every task.

The task in front of me deserves all of me.

I remind myself: when I split my attention, I weaken my power. If I'm thinking about the past while I'm working in the present, I rob myself. If I'm dreaming about the future while ignoring the now, I sabotage myself.

Presence is where my strength lives. Every task — big or small — deserves my full focus. Washing dishes, writing words, having a conversation — when I give it everything, I become sharper, stronger, more alive.

Presence is not about perfection; it's about respect. Respect for my time. Respect for my effort. Respect for the moment I will never get back. When I am fully present, life feels deeper, and my work becomes cleaner.

I will not drift through my days half-alive. I will stay present in every task — because how I do the small things creates how I do the big things.

Gem of Knowledge

Presence turns ordinary tasks into training for greatness.

Reflection 25: I prepare before the battle begins.

Victory is won long before the fight starts.

I remind myself: the battle doesn't begin the moment I step into it — it begins in my preparation. If I wait until the pressure comes, I'm already behind. But if I prepare beforehand, I enter with strength already built.

Preparation is my shield. It is my strategy. It is my advantage over those who only react when the challenge arrives. When others scramble, I'm steady. When others panic, I'm ready.

That means I do the work no one sees. I train in silence. I study while others sleep. I sharpen my skills when no one's watching. And when the battle finally arrives, I don't have to pretend — I perform.

The outcome is often decided before the first step, the first swing, the first move. And I will never walk into a fight unprepared.

Gem of Knowledge

I win not in the moment of battle, but in the moments before it.

Reflection 26: I do not drown in overthinking.

Overthinking is quicksand — the more I struggle in it, the deeper I sink.

I remind myself: thinking is a tool, but overthinking is a trap. My mind wants to replay every mistake, imagine every scenario, predict every outcome. It feels like progress, but it's not. It's paralysis.

When I overthink, I remind myself to stop chasing control. I will never know every answer. I will never predict every twist. And that's okay. My job isn't to solve the whole puzzle at once — it's to take the next piece and place it.

Instead of drowning in endless thought, I move. I act. I choose. Even if the step isn't perfect, it pulls me out of the trap of hesitation. Action cuts through the fog that thought alone cannot clear.

My mind is meant to serve me, not suffocate me. I refuse to sink in the weight of overthinking. I rise through movement, clarity, and trust in the moment.

Gem of Knowledge

Overthinking kills progress; action revives it.

Reflection 27: I am relentless in focus.

Focus is not a mood — it's a decision I make again and again.

I remind myself: distractions will always exist. The world is designed to scatter me, to pull me in a hundred directions at once. But focus is my rebellion. Focus is my power.

Being relentless in focus means I don't just try once and quit. It means I bring my attention back every time it drifts. Over and over, I choose what matters most. That's how I outlast everyone else.

I don't give my focus to what doesn't serve me. I don't scatter it on meaningless noise. I cut deep into the task at hand until it's done, until it's real, until it's undeniable.

Relentless focus is how I build momentum. It's how I turn small steps into unstoppable results. My future is not built on intensity once in a while — it's built on sustained focus, again and again.

Gem of Knowledge

Relentless focus makes me unstoppable.

Reflection 28: I shape my mind through discipline.

Discipline is the sculptor; my mind is the stone.

I remind myself: my mind is not fixed. It can be shaped, molded, sharpened. But it will not shape itself. If I leave it alone, it grows wild. If I discipline it, it becomes powerful.

Discipline is not punishment — it's design. It's me deciding what thoughts stay and what thoughts go. It's me saying *no* to impulses that weaken me and *yes* to habits that strengthen me.

Every time I wake up early when I want to sleep in, every time I choose growth over comfort, every time I control my mind instead of letting it control me — I carve another piece off the stone. Slowly, day by day, the masterpiece of who I am meant to be is revealed.

I am not waiting for discipline to magically appear. I choose it daily. Because discipline is the hand that sculpts my mind into greatness.

Gem of Knowledge

Discipline shapes me into who I was born to be.

Reflection 29: I control the story I tell myself.

The story I repeat becomes the life I live.

I remind myself: my mind is always narrating. It tells stories about who I am, what I can do, and what my life means. If I don't take control of that story, it will control me.

If I tell myself I'm weak, I'll live weak. If I tell myself I'm broken, I'll stay broken. But if I tell myself I'm strong, if I tell myself I'm capable, if I tell myself I can endure and rise — then my life bends to that story.

I don't lie to myself. I don't sugarcoat. But I choose to speak truth in a way that builds me instead of breaks me. I am not the victim of my story — I am the author. I decide the tone. I decide the ending.

Every day I have a choice: repeat the story that keeps me small or write the story that makes me rise. And I will always choose the story that makes me stronger.

Gem of Knowledge

I am the author of the story I live.

31

Reflection 30: I release what I cannot control.

Holding on to what I can't change only chains me.

I remind myself: not everything is mine to carry. Life is full of people, events, and outcomes I can't control. The more I grip them, the more they drain me. Worrying doesn't fix them. Obsessing doesn't move them. It only steals my peace.

Releasing is not weakness — it's wisdom. It's knowing where my power begins and where it ends. I cannot control other people's choices. I cannot control every twist of fate. But I can control how I respond, how I show up, and how I protect my energy.

When I release what is not mine, I reclaim my strength for what is. My focus returns. My mind clears. My body breathes easier. I don't waste life wrestling with what I was never meant to hold.

Freedom comes when I unclench my grip and let go.

Gem of Knowledge

Letting go of what I can't control gives me power over what I can.

Reflection 31: My self-talk builds me, not breaks me.

The loudest voice I hear all day is my own.

I remind myself: words matter, especially the ones I speak to myself. If I talk to myself like an enemy, I will live like I'm under attack. If I talk to myself like a friend, I will rise with strength.

I cannot escape my own voice. It follows me into every decision, every challenge, every moment of doubt. So I make it my ally. I speak words that build, not words that tear down. I speak to myself the way I would speak to someone I love — with truth, with strength, with encouragement.

This doesn't mean I avoid honesty. It means my honesty carries purpose. Instead of saying, *"I can't do this,"* I say, *"This will be hard, but I am capable."* Instead of, *"I always fail,"* I say, *"I'm learning, and I'm still moving forward."*

My self-talk is not background noise — it is construction. Every word I choose either builds my future or breaks it apart. And I will only build.

Gem of Knowledge

My self-talk is my foundation — I choose to build, not destroy.

33

Reflection 32: I do not indulge negative spirals.

One negative thought can become a storm if I feed it.

I remind myself: negativity has a way of multiplying. One bad thought triggers another, and another, until I'm trapped in a spiral that feels endless. But I am not powerless — I decide whether the spiral lives or dies.

The moment I catch myself sinking, I stop. I breathe. I break the cycle. I don't indulge it, I don't fuel it, I don't give it more energy than it deserves. Instead, I redirect. I move, I act, I shift my focus onto something that builds me.

The spiral only grows if I feed it. If I starve it, it dies. I remind myself that I have power over what I repeat. I do not give negativity free rent in my mind.

Strength is not about never feeling negative. Strength is about refusing to spiral when it shows up.

Gem of Knowledge

Negativity only spirals if I feed it — and I refuse to feed it.

Reflection 33: I am alert, aware, and awake.

Life is happening right now — I refuse to sleep through it.

I remind myself: too many people live half-asleep. They go through the motions. They scroll, they drift, they repeat yesterday without noticing today. But not me. I train myself to be alert, aware, and awake.

Being alert means I see what others miss. I notice the details, the shifts, the opportunities. Being aware means I don't just move blindly — I recognize how my choices shape my life. And being awake means I don't live on autopilot. I choose my steps with intention.

When I'm fully awake, the world feels sharper. The small things matter more. The big things don't scare me as much. I move with clarity because I'm not lost in distraction.

This is the life I want — not a half-lived one, but a conscious one. One where I see clearly, act decisively, and remain fully present in every moment.

Gem of Knowledge

Awareness turns life from routine into power.

Reflection 34: I feed my mind with strength.

My mind becomes what I feed it.

I remind myself: my mind is always hungry. If I don't choose what to feed it, the world will. And the world feeds junk — negativity, fear, gossip, weakness. If I consume that, it becomes who I am.

So I choose strength. I feed my mind with words that build, stories that inspire, truths that sharpen me. I feed it with discipline, with wisdom, with reminders of who I want to become.

Just like the body grows from what I eat, my mind grows from what I consume. If I want strength, I must feed it strength. If I want clarity, I must feed it clarity.

Every book I read, every conversation I choose, every thought I repeat — they're meals for my mind. And I refuse to feed it poison. I only feed it what makes me powerful.

Gem of Knowledge

What I feed my mind becomes the strength I live.

Reflection 35: My thoughts are tools, not prisons.

Thoughts are meant to serve me, not sentence me.

I remind myself: thoughts are powerful, but they are not chains. Too often, I let them trap me — *"I'm not ready," "I can't do this," "I always fail."* These are not facts. They are tools gone unused; weapons pointed at me instead of for me.

A thought is only as strong as the power I give it. If I treat it as a command, it enslaves me. But if I treat it as a tool, I can use it to build, to solve, to grow.

I don't let my thoughts imprison me anymore. I don't sit behind the bars of doubt, fear, or regret. Instead, I grab hold of my thoughts and put them to work. They're hammers, not handcuffs. They're chisels, not cages.

My thoughts do not own me. I own them. And I will use them to carve the life I want, not the prison I don't.

Gem of Knowledge

Thoughts build when I use them — they trap me only if I obey them.

Reflection 36: I never stop learning.

The day I stop learning is the day I stop living.

I remind myself: growth is endless. The world never stops moving, and neither can I. If I stop learning, I fall behind. If I stop growing, I shrink.

Learning is not just about books — it's about life. Every mistake, every conversation, every challenge is a lesson if I'm awake enough to see it. And every lesson makes me stronger.

I don't let pride blind me into thinking I know enough. I don't let fear keep me from seeking new truths. I stay open, I stay curious, I stay hungry. Because the mind that never stops learning is the mind that never gets trapped.

Every day is an opportunity to expand. Every day is a chance to discover something that changes everything. I will not waste that gift.

Gem of Knowledge

As long as I keep learning, I keep rising.

Reflection 37: My mental clarity is my weapon.

In a world of noise, clarity cuts deeper than strength.

I remind myself: power is not just muscle, not just money, not just noise. Power is clarity. The ability to see through the fog when others are blinded. The ability to act with precision when others are paralyzed.

My clarity is not accidental — I train it. I sharpen it by removing distractions, by quieting my mind, by refusing to let the world's noise control me. When my mind is clear, I don't waste energy on confusion. I don't waste time on doubt. I act with direction.

Clarity makes me dangerous to anything that tries to stop me. Because while others are lost in chaos, I see the path forward. While others hesitate, I move.

I will not live in the fog. I choose to live sharp, awake, and precise. My clarity is my advantage, my edge, my weapon.

Gem of Knowledge

Clarity cuts through what confusion cannot.

Reflection 38: I trust the power of preparation.

The work I do in silence becomes my victory in public.

I remind myself: talent is nothing without preparation. Desire is nothing without readiness. The future belongs to those who prepare before the moment arrives.

Preparation is my secret weapon. It's why I study when no one's watching. It's why I practice the details others ignore. It's why I put in effort now, before anyone asks for it. Because I know the battle is won before it begins.

When I prepare, I walk into challenges with confidence. I don't rely on luck. I don't scramble at the last second. I show up already armed, already ready, already strong. And that gives me peace.

I trust preparation because it never betrays me. Every ounce of work I put in beforehand comes back multiplied when it matters most. I win not by chance, but by choice — the choice to prepare.

Gem of Knowledge

Preparation turns uncertainty into confidence.

Reflection 39: I challenge every lazy thought.

Laziness whispers comfort; I answer with challenge.

I remind myself: laziness always sounds tempting. It says, *"Rest more, do it later, skip it just this once."* But I know the truth — laziness is not rest, it's decay. Rest restores me. Laziness rots me.

So every time a lazy thought shows up, I challenge it. I ask: *Will this choice make me stronger or weaker? Will this step move me closer or push me back?* And when I see the truth, I choose the harder road — because the harder road makes me greater.

Laziness doesn't show up as a monster. It shows up as comfort. But comfort kills potential. And I will not trade my future for a few minutes of ease.

I rise when I don't want to. I move when it feels easier to stay still. I work when my mind begs me to quit. Because greatness isn't built in the moments of motivation — it's built in the moments when I defeat laziness.

Gem of Knowledge

Laziness offers ease; challenge builds me.

Reflection 40: I choose logic over impulse.

Impulse is noise. Logic is power.

I remind myself: impulses are fast, loud, and reckless. They scream at me to react, to chase, to grab what feels good right now. But impulse is short-term fire that burns me out. Logic is steady flame that lights my way.

When impulse says, *"Quit now,"* logic says, *"Stay — you're almost there."* When impulse says, *"Spend it all,"* logic says, *"Save and build."* When impulse says, *"React in anger,"* logic says, *"Pause — don't ruin your peace."*

Logic is not emotionless; it's wise. It's me stepping back to see the whole picture before moving. It's me refusing to let temporary feelings destroy permanent goals.

Every time I choose logic over impulse, I take control of my life. I stop being a slave to moods and start being a master of decisions. Impulse is easy. Logic is powerful. And I always choose power.

Gem of Knowledge

Impulse is noise; logic is my compass.

Reflection 41: My mind bends but does not break.

Pressure may bend me, but it will never break me.

I remind myself: life will test me. The weight will come. Circumstances will stretch me beyond what I thought I could handle. Some days will feel like I'm at the breaking point. But I am not fragile. I am flexible. My mind bends, but it does not break.

When I bend, I adapt. I adjust. I find a way to move with the storm instead of against it. Bending doesn't mean I've lost strength — it means I've found endurance. Trees that never bend snap in the wind. The strongest ones sway, and because of that, they survive.

My mind works the same. It may shake under pressure, but it will not collapse. It finds ways to bend, to shift, to keep me moving forward even when everything seems against me. And when the storm passes — as it always does — I rise again, stronger than before.

So I do not fear the moments that test me. They don't break me — they prove me.

Gem of Knowledge

Flexibility under pressure is not weakness — it is resilience.

Reflection 42: I train focus like a muscle.

Focus grows stronger every time I practice it.

I remind myself: focus is not something I'm born with. It's not something that just "happens." Focus is a muscle — and like any muscle, it grows when I train it.

Every time I bring my attention back from distraction, I'm lifting mental weight. Every time I sit down and stay with a task longer than I want to, I'm adding another rep. Every time I refuse to scatter my attention, I'm building strength.

Just like in the gym, consistency matters more than intensity. I don't need to be perfect. I don't need to focus for hours without drifting. I just need to keep training, keep returning, keep building. Over time, my focus becomes unshakable.

This is why others give up while I keep going. They never trained their focus. They let distractions rule them. But I have practiced, and because of that, I have power. Focus gives me clarity. Focus gives me progress. Focus builds my future.

Gem of Knowledge

The more I train my focus, the heavier goals I can lift.

Reflection 43: I sharpen wisdom through reflection.

Experience teaches nothing if I don't reflect on it.

I remind myself: wisdom is not just living through things — it's learning from them. People repeat the same mistakes for years because they never stop to reflect. They keep moving, but they don't grow. I refuse to live that way.

Reflection is my sharpening stone. When I look back on my choices, my wins, my losses, I see the patterns. I see where I was strong, and I see where I was blind. Reflection turns mistakes into lessons. It turns victories into blueprints. It turns my life into a teacher.

But reflection isn't about regret. It's about growth. It's about asking myself: *What did I learn? How will I apply it? How can I move forward better than before?* With every reflection, my wisdom sharpens.

I don't rush past my experiences. I pause, I reflect, and I grow. And because of that, every step I take carries more wisdom than the one before.

Gem of Knowledge

Reflection turns life into a teacher and wisdom into a weapon.

Reflection 44: I master boredom with discipline.

Boredom is not my enemy — it is my training ground.

I remind myself: most people quit when things get boring. They want excitement, constant stimulation, instant results. But mastery is built in the boring. Discipline is forged in the repetition that feels dull, in the work no one claps for.

Boredom is not weakness; boredom is a test. It asks me, *Will you keep showing up even when it's not exciting? Will you stay the course even when no one's watching?* My answer is yes.

I master boredom by embracing it. I lean into the quiet, the routine, the grind. Because I know greatness is not built on flashes of inspiration — it's built on consistency. And consistency means doing the work whether I feel thrilled or tired, whether the task is glamorous or dull.

Discipline turns boredom into progress. Every rep, every page, every hour spent repeating the basics is carving strength into me. I don't escape boredom — I master it.

Gem of Knowledge

Boredom is where most quit, but where I grow.

48

Reflection 45: I think strategically, not emotionally.

Emotion reacts. Strategy wins.

I remind myself: emotions are powerful, but they are unstable. They can make me explode when I should wait. They can make me retreat when I should advance. If I let emotions lead me, I lose.

Strategy is my compass. Strategy steps back, sees the whole board, and makes the move that serves me long-term. Thinking strategically means I don't trade the future for a feeling. I don't let anger, fear, or excitement push me into decisions that weaken me.

This doesn't mean I deny my emotions. It means I don't hand them the steering wheel. I let them speak, but strategy makes the call.

When I think strategically, I win the long game. I don't just react to what's in front of me — I plan for what's ahead. I build, I position, I move with intention. Emotion is noise; strategy is strength.

Gem of Knowledge

I feel my emotions, but I follow my strategy.

Reflection 46: I don't seek easy answers.

Easy answers comfort me but never change me.

I remind myself: the world is full of shortcuts, simple fixes, and quick escapes. But every easy answer comes with a hidden cost. It keeps me weak. It keeps me blind. It keeps me from growth.

Real answers are not easy — they're earned. They require thought, reflection, discipline, and often pain. But they're the answers that last. They're the ones that build me into someone who cannot be shaken.

When my mind wants quick relief, I resist. When I want instant solutions, I stop and ask: *What is the real truth here? What is the harder path that will make me greater?*

I remind myself: growth does not come from comfort. It comes from challenge. Easy answers are traps; hard truths are freedom. And I choose freedom.

Gem of Knowledge

I don't chase easy answers — I earn lasting truths.

Reflection 47: My thoughts align with my purpose.

If my thoughts don't serve my purpose, I replace them.

I remind myself: every thought I hold either pushes me toward my purpose or pulls me away from it. There is no neutral. My mind must align with what I am here to do.

When I catch myself thinking small, I redirect. When I catch myself doubting, I refocus. I remind myself: *This thought does not serve me. This thought does not belong here.* And then I choose one that aligns with who I am becoming.

Alignment is discipline. It's not about never having weak thoughts — it's about refusing to live in them. It's about choosing again and again to feed the thoughts that give me strength, vision, and direction.

My purpose is too important to be sabotaged by random noise in my mind. I choose alignment. I choose strength. I choose thoughts that build the life I came here to live.

Gem of Knowledge

I align my thoughts with purpose, not with fear.

Reflection 48: I remove noise to hear truth.

Truth doesn't shout — it whispers beneath the noise.

I remind myself: the world is loud. Opinions, headlines, distractions, and endless chatter compete for my attention. If I'm not careful, I mistake noise for truth. But truth lives in silence.

When I quiet the noise, I hear my own voice again. I hear wisdom. I hear clarity. I hear the difference between what I truly want and what the world wants for me.

Removing noise is not about escaping life — it's about filtering it. It's choosing what deserves to enter my mind and what does not. It's turning down the voices of doubt, comparison, and distraction so I can hear what actually matters.

The truth is never complicated. It's simple. But I can only hear it when I create the space for it. That's why I remove the noise. That's why I protect my silence. Because in the quiet, the truth rises.

Gem of Knowledge

Noise confuses me; silence reveals truth.

Reflection 49: I keep my mind sharp through struggle.

Struggle is not dulling me — it is sharpening me.

I remind myself: struggle is not here to destroy me. Struggle is the grindstone that sharpens my mind. Every challenge, every obstacle, every setback forces me to think clearer, act smarter, and become stronger.

When life is easy, my edge dulls. Comfort softens me. But when struggle shows up, I grow sharper. I adapt. I problem-solve. I find strength in places I didn't know I had.

I don't run from struggle anymore. I lean into it. Because I know that every hardship is training. Every problem is shaping me into someone who cannot be broken easily.

Sharpness doesn't come from rest alone — it comes from resistance. Struggle is not my enemy. It is the whetstone that keeps my mind ready for anything.

Gem of Knowledge

Struggle sharpens me into who I must become.

53

Reflection 50: I don't react; I respond with clarity.

Reaction is impulse; response is power.

I remind myself: reacting is easy. It's quick, it's emotional, it's reckless. But reacting makes me a slave to the moment. Responding makes me master of it.

When something triggers me, I pause. I breathe. I give myself the space to see clearly before I move. That pause is my power. It keeps me from speaking words I'll regret, from making choices that weaken me.

Clarity doesn't mean moving slowly — it means moving wisely. It means stepping back long enough to see the whole picture before stepping forward with purpose.

I will not let emotions, impulses, or outside pressure control me. I will respond with clarity, with strength, with intention. Because my response defines me, not my reaction.

Gem of Knowledge

Reaction is noise; clarity is command.

Reflection 51: My inner dialogue is disciplined.

The way I speak to myself shapes the way I live.

I remind myself: my inner voice never stops talking. It's with me when I wake, when I work, when I rest. If that voice is undisciplined, it can destroy me. If it is disciplined, it can build me into someone unshakable.

Discipline in my inner dialogue means I don't allow chaos inside. I don't let self-pity run wild. I don't let negativity spiral. I choose words that correct me, strengthen me, and guide me. I speak to myself with honesty, but also with power.

Every disciplined word is a brick. Day by day, I build an inner fortress where I can stand tall, no matter what storms rage outside. I don't let my voice be careless. I use it with precision, because it is shaping my life from the inside out.

Gem of Knowledge

Discipline in my voice creates discipline in my life.

Reflection 52: I own my mind, fully and completely.

If I don't own my mind, the world will.

I remind myself: my mind is my greatest territory. It is the space where my life begins. If I don't claim it, everything else will. Distractions will own it. Fear will own it. Other people's voices will own it. And I refuse to live like that.

Owning my mind means taking full responsibility. I decide what thoughts stay. I decide what beliefs remain. I decide what voices I let in and what lies I throw out. Nothing enters my mind without my permission.

Ownership is not a one-time act — it's daily discipline. Every morning, I take command. Every night, I guard the gates. Because I know the quality of my mind determines the quality of my life.

I am not a visitor in my own head. I am the ruler. And I will not surrender this throne to fear, doubt, or distraction.

Gem of Knowledge

When I own my mind, I own my life.

Reflection 53: I do what must be done, not what I feel like.

Feelings don't build my future — actions do.

I remind myself: my feelings are temporary. They rise, they fall, they shift with the day. One moment I feel strong, the next I feel tired, the next I don't want to move at all. If I let my feelings lead, I'll live on a rollercoaster that goes nowhere.

Discipline is doing what must be done, no matter how I feel. It's showing up when I'm tired. It's working when I'd rather rest. It's pushing when my emotions tell me to quit. Because my future doesn't care how I feel — it only reflects what I do.

The days I don't feel like it are the days that matter most. Those are the days that separate the weak from the strong. Anybody can work when it's easy. I rise when it's hard.

Gem of Knowledge

Feelings pass — discipline remains.

Reflection 54: My emotions serve me; they do not control me.

I feel my emotions, but I don't bow to them.

I remind myself: emotions are not enemies. They are signals, messages, indicators of what's happening inside me. Anger says something feels wrong. Fear says something feels risky. Sadness says something feels lost. These are signals, not commands.

I let my emotions serve me, but I do not hand them the wheel. Anger sharpens my awareness, but I respond with strategy. Fear reminds me to be cautious, but I move forward anyway. Sadness shows me what I value, but I don't stay stuck in it.

This is mastery: to feel deeply, but not be ruled by what I feel. To use my emotions as tools, not chains. To remain free even while I feel fully.

Gem of Knowledge

Emotions inform me — they don't govern me.

Reflection 55: Pain is feedback, not a reason to quit.

Pain is not punishment — it's instruction.

I remind myself: pain is not proof that I'm failing. Pain is proof that I'm stretching, growing, being tested. It is feedback — a message telling me to pay attention.

Pain says, *"Adjust your form."* Pain says, *"This is your edge — now push it."* Pain says, *"Here's where you're weak — strengthen it."* If I run from pain, I run from growth. If I listen to it, I learn from it.

Most people quit at the first sign of discomfort. But I refuse to mistake pain for defeat. Pain is not the end. It is the beginning of transformation.

So I lean into it. I don't let it stop me. I let it sharpen me.

Gem of Knowledge

Pain isn't a wall — it's a teacher.

Reflection 56: I rise faster than I fall.

Falling is not failure — staying down is.

I remind myself: I will fall. I will stumble. I will fail. That's part of life, part of growth, part of building anything that matters. The question is not whether I fall — it's how quickly I rise.

When I hit the ground, I don't waste time in self-pity. I don't replay the mistake endlessly. I rise. And the faster I rise, the less power the fall has over me.

Every comeback makes me stronger. Every quick rise teaches me that no failure can keep me down. Falling may be natural, but rising is my choice. And I choose to rise every time.

Gem of Knowledge

Falling humbles me — rising defines me.

Reflection 57: Every day I train the muscle of discipline.

Discipline is not a gift — it's a muscle I build daily.

I remind myself: no one is born disciplined. No one wakes up with unshakable habits or perfect consistency. Discipline is built the same way strength is built — through training, repetition, and practice.

Every time I follow through on a commitment, I lift that weight. Every time I keep going when I'd rather quit, I add another rep. Every time I resist comfort to choose growth, I make the muscle stronger.

I know the days I don't want to show up are the most important. Those are the heavy reps. Those are the sets that matter. Because discipline doesn't grow when it's easy. It grows when it's hard, when I resist the urge to stop, when I push myself past the point of "enough."

So every day I train. Some days I succeed, some days I stumble, but I never stop. And because of that, my discipline grows into something most people never have — unshakable strength.

Gem of Knowledge

Discipline grows when I train it daily, not when I wait for it.

Reflection 58: I master the small choices that shape my life.

The small choices I make in silence decide the life I live in public.

I remind myself: it's not just the big moments that define me — it's the small ones. The little choices, the quiet decisions, the habits repeated daily. Each one seems small, but they stack into a life.

When I choose to get up instead of sleep in — that shapes me. When I choose water over junk, reading over scrolling, effort over laziness — that shapes me. Every small choice adds up to a pattern. And the pattern becomes my life.

Most people wait for the big moments to prove themselves. But big moments are only the reflection of small choices made daily. If I master the small, I'll master the big automatically.

I take pride in the little wins. Because I know every step, every choice, every small act of discipline becomes part of the person I'm building.

Gem of Knowledge

Small choices, repeated daily, build my destiny.

Reflection 59: I face discomfort; that is where growth lives.

Comfort never changed me — discomfort always did.

I remind myself: growth and comfort cannot live in the same place. If I choose comfort, I choose stagnation. If I choose discomfort, I choose growth. It has always been that way.

Discomfort is the doorway to strength. The workout that burns, the conversation that scares me, the risk that challenges me — these are the moments that expand me. Every time I face discomfort instead of running, I grow.

I don't wait for comfort anymore. I don't look for the easy road. I lean into the stretch, the strain, the hard moments. Because I know that's where the transformation happens. That's where the old me breaks and the new me begins.

I am not afraid of discomfort. I welcome it. Because every time I face it, I walk out stronger.

Gem of Knowledge

Discomfort is not pain — it is proof of growth.

Reflection 60: My actions prove my words.

Words mean nothing until action makes them real.

I remind myself: talk is cheap. Promises are easy. Everyone can say what they'll do, who they'll become, what they want to achieve. But without action, words are empty air.

My actions are my proof. My habits, my discipline, my follow-through — they speak louder than anything I could ever say. If I say I want change, I show it by changing. If I say I want growth, I prove it by putting in the work.

I remind myself: my reputation, my results, my legacy will not be built on what I said I'd do. They'll be built on what I actually did.

So I don't waste time convincing people with my words. I convince them with my consistency. I let my actions speak, because they can never lie.

Gem of Knowledge

My actions are my voice — they prove who I am.

Reflection 61: I don't need easy; I need progress.

Easy doesn't change me — progress does.

I remind myself: life is not meant to be easy. Easy keeps me still. Easy keeps me small. Easy may feel good for a moment, but it leaves me unchanged. Progress, on the other hand, stretches me. Progress demands more. Progress transforms me.

When I look back, I don't remember the easy days. I remember the struggles I overcame, the hard choices I made, the growth that came from pain. That's where pride lives. That's where strength comes from.

So I don't pray for easy. I don't chase it. I don't waste energy wishing things were smoother, lighter, simpler. I want progress. I want growth. I want to climb the mountain, not sit at the bottom wishing it were shorter.

Progress is all I need. Because progress builds the future, not ease.

Gem of Knowledge

Easy changes nothing — progress changes everything.

Reflection 62: Weakness dies in my persistence.

Persistence kills weakness one step at a time.

I remind myself: weakness only wins when I quit. But if I keep going, even slowly, even imperfectly, weakness cannot survive.

Persistence is not glamorous. It's not flashy. It's repetition. It's refusing to stop. It's showing up again and again, even when I don't feel strong, even when I don't feel motivated. Every step I take while weak is another blow against my weakness.

Persistence doesn't mean I never fall. It means I never stay down. It means I return, I push, I endure until weakness has no power left.

I remind myself: weakness fades in the face of persistence. Strength rises where persistence lives.

Gem of Knowledge

Weakness dies the moment I refuse to quit.

Reflection 63: I do not wait for motivation — I act without it.

Motivation is a luxury — action is a necessity.

I remind myself: motivation is unreliable. Some days it's there, most days it isn't. If I wait for motivation, I'll wait forever. The ones who win are not the ones who feel motivated — they're the ones who act without it.

I move whether I feel inspired or not. I put in the work whether my energy is high or low. I show up because the action matters more than the mood.

Ironically, I've learned this truth: action creates motivation. The moment I start, the energy follows. The moment I move, momentum builds. Waiting for motivation is weakness; creating momentum is strength.

So I don't wait for the right feeling. I build the right feeling by acting first.

Gem of Knowledge

Motivation fades — action endures.

Reflection 64: I endure what others avoid.

What others run from, I face — and that's why I grow stronger.

I remind myself: most people avoid the hard road. They run from struggle, from discipline, from the grind. They want comfort, shortcuts, and ease. But comfort never made anyone great.

I endure what others avoid. I face the pain, the repetition, the pressure, the silence. Because I know those are the very things that shape me. Endurance is my edge. It allows me to keep walking long after others have quit.

When discomfort rises, I don't see it as punishment. I see it as proof that I'm on the right path. Struggle is the filter that separates the weak from the strong. And I choose to go where others refuse to go.

I remind myself: anyone can walk the easy road. Few endure the hard one. But the hard one builds me into someone unshakable. That's why I keep walking. That's why I endure.

Gem of Knowledge

Endurance in what others avoid makes me unstoppable.

Reflection 65: Success is built on my habits, not my feelings.

Feelings change by the hour — habits shape my life forever.

I remind myself: feelings are unstable. They shift with the weather, the mood, the moment. One day I feel unstoppable, the next I feel heavy and slow. If I build my life on feelings, my foundation will always crumble.

But habits — habits are steady. They are the small daily actions that repeat no matter how I feel. Waking up early. Staying consistent. Keeping promises to myself. These are bricks I lay day after day, until they build the structure of success.

The truth is, habits don't care how I feel. They only care whether I do them. And that's why they're so powerful — they remove the guesswork, the drama, the hesitation. If I've built the right habits, I don't need to think. I just act.

So I don't chase feelings anymore. I build habits. Because I know my future is written not by how I feel in a moment, but by what I do every day.

Gem of Knowledge

Feelings fade — habits last.

Reflection 66: I sharpen my mind by mastering my body.

A weak body clouds the mind; a strong body sharpens it.

I remind myself: my mind and body are not separate. When my body is undisciplined, my mind suffers. When my body is trained, my mind becomes sharper.

Every workout is not just physical — it's mental training. Every time I push through exhaustion, I strengthen not just my muscles but my willpower. Every time I demand discipline from my body, my mind learns endurance, focus, and clarity.

A neglected body breeds weakness in thought. Laziness in movement creates laziness in spirit. But a trained body builds confidence, resilience, and sharpness of mind.

So I move. I train. I push. Not just for health, but for mastery. Because every drop of sweat sharpens me inside and out.

Gem of Knowledge

A disciplined body creates a disciplined mind.

Reflection 67: I am stronger than my excuses.

Excuses are lies — strength is truth.

I remind myself: excuses sound convincing, but they are nothing more than permission to stay weak. *I'm too tired. I don't have time. It's not the right moment.* These are traps dressed up as reasons.

But I am stronger than my excuses. I know every time I defeat one, I prove it has no real power. Excuses only live if I feed them. The moment I act despite them, they vanish.

Strength is not about never feeling like quitting — it's about refusing to let the excuse be the last word. I hear it, I recognize it, and then I crush it by moving forward anyway.

My excuses are clever, but my will is stronger. And as long as I keep choosing strength, no excuse will ever own me.

Gem of Knowledge

Excuses die the moment I act.

Reflection 68: Failure is my teacher, not my identity.

Failure does not define me — it instructs me.

I remind myself: everyone fails. Everyone falls short. The difference is how they see it. Some take failure as proof they are worthless. Others take it as feedback to grow.

Failure is not my identity. It does not say who I am. It only says where I need to adjust, improve, or try again. Failure is a mirror showing me the truth, not a chain holding me back.

When I fail, I ask: *What is this teaching me? How can I use this? Where do I need to change?* And when I answer those questions, failure becomes fuel. It shapes me, strengthens me, and sets me up for success.

I don't fear failure anymore. I welcome it, because I know it carries the lessons that comfort never will.

Gem of Knowledge

Failure is feedback — not identity.

Reflection 69: I control what I give my attention to.

My attention is my currency — I spend it wisely.

I remind myself: the world is fighting for my attention. Every ad, every headline, every distraction is designed to steal it. But my attention is not free. It is the most valuable thing I own, and I decide where it goes.

If I give my attention to fear, fear grows. If I give it to gossip, gossip grows. If I give it to my vision, my vision grows. What I feed with focus becomes my future.

That means I must guard it carefully. I must choose who and what deserves it. I must cut out distractions that drain me and give more to the things that build me.

I remind myself daily: I control my attention, not the world. And because of that, I control my destiny.

Gem of Knowledge

What I focus on expands — so I choose with intention.

Reflection 70: My word is a contract with myself.

If I can't trust my own word, I can't trust anything.

I remind myself: when I speak, my words are not casual. They are promises, contracts, commitments — especially the ones I make to myself. Every time I break my own word, I weaken my foundation. Every time I keep it, I build unshakable trust in myself.

Most people are quick to honor promises to others but careless with promises to themselves. They'll show up for everyone else, but abandon their own goals, their own commitments, their own dreams. I refuse to live that way.

When I say I'll do something, I do it — even if no one is watching. Especially if no one is watching. Because it's not about proving to others. It's about proving to myself that I am reliable, that my word is law.

My confidence is not built on hype. It's built on evidence — evidence that I can trust myself because I honor my own contracts.

Gem of Knowledge

Every kept promise to myself is a brick of self-trust.

Reflection 71: I don't seek comfort — I create strength.

Comfort keeps me soft; strength carries me forward.

I remind myself: the world tells me to chase comfort, to seek ease, to avoid hardship. But I know comfort never built anything worth keeping. Comfort makes me weak. Strength makes me unstoppable.

That's why I don't chase comfort. I create strength. I choose the harder path, the disciplined road, the one that stretches me. Because I know strength is forged in the places where comfort dies.

Strength is not just about muscles or endurance — it's about character. It's about doing what others won't. It's about building resilience that can't be broken by small storms. Comfort avoids the fire; strength is shaped by it.

I don't fear discomfort. I use it. Because every time I endure what is hard, I become stronger than the one who chose the easy way.

Gem of Knowledge

Comfort fades — strength remains.

77

Reflection 72: I am unshaken by setbacks.

Setbacks don't move me — they sharpen me.

I remind myself: setbacks are part of the journey. They are not proof that I've failed; they are proof that I'm trying. Everyone stumbles. Everyone faces resistance. But I refuse to let setbacks shake me.

When something knocks me off course, I don't collapse. I adjust. I learn. I get back on track. The difference between those who fail and those who succeed is not that one never faced setbacks — it's that one refused to be defined by them.

Setbacks are not signs to quit. They are reminders that I am in the fight. They are checkpoints on the road to growth. And every time I rise through one, I become stronger than before.

So when I hit a wall, I don't break. I climb. I adapt. I keep moving. I am unshaken.

Gem of Knowledge

Setbacks don't stop me — they sharpen me.

Reflection 73: Discipline is freedom; I practice it daily.

Without discipline, I am trapped. With discipline, I am free.

I remind myself: discipline is not restriction — it is freedom. Without it, I am chained to moods, impulses, distractions, and weakness. With it, I am free to build the life I want, not just the life my feelings allow.

Discipline gives me control. It allows me to say no to what weakens me and yes to what strengthens me. It gives me the power to move forward even when everything in me wants to quit.

But discipline is not built in a single act — it's practiced daily. Every morning I wake up and choose it. Every decision, every choice, every habit is another opportunity to practice. Some days I stumble, but the practice never ends.

Discipline gives me freedom because it makes me master of myself. And mastery is the highest form of liberty.

Gem of Knowledge

Discipline costs me comfort, but it buys me freedom.

Reflection 74: My future bows to my daily choices.

The future is not luck — it is the echo of my daily choices.

I remind myself: tomorrow is not random. My future is not decided by chance. It is built, piece by piece, by the choices I make today. Every action compounds. Every decision adds weight. Every small move builds momentum toward what's coming.

If I want a strong future, I make strong choices now. If I want peace, I choose discipline over chaos. If I want success, I choose consistency over comfort. My future is not waiting to surprise me — it's waiting to mirror me.

I don't control everything that happens to me, but I control my choices. And my choices are powerful enough to shape what tomorrow looks like.

So I live with awareness. I choose carefully. Because I know my future will bow to the decisions I make today.

Gem of Knowledge

My future is not luck — it is my choices multiplied.

Reflection 75: I am consistent, not perfect.

Perfection is impossible — consistency is unstoppable.

I remind myself: chasing perfection is a trap. It keeps me frozen, waiting until I can do it flawlessly. But life doesn't reward perfection — it rewards consistency.

Consistency means showing up again and again, even when it's messy, even when it's hard, even when it doesn't feel like enough. It's the daily effort, not the flawless one, that builds results.

When I miss, I don't quit. I return. When I stumble, I don't stop. I keep moving. Because consistency is not about never failing — it's about always coming back.

I know perfection doesn't exist, but consistency does. And consistency is stronger, because it creates momentum that perfection could never touch.

Gem of Knowledge

Perfection is fragile — consistency is unstoppable.

Reflection 76: I create order in my mind and my life.

Chaos outside doesn't mean chaos inside — I choose order.

I remind myself: the world is messy, unpredictable, and full of noise. But I don't have to let that same chaos live inside me. Order begins in my mind. And when I create order in my mind, my life begins to follow.

I choose clarity over clutter. I choose structure over disorder. I choose to align my thoughts, my priorities, my actions, so they point in one direction — forward. When I create mental order, I cut through the confusion that stops most people.

My life is a reflection of my inner world. If I'm scattered inside, I'll be scattered outside. If I'm steady inside, I can bring order to everything around me. I don't wait for things to "get better." I bring order with my discipline, my choices, and my focus.

Order is not rigidity — it is strength. It is me shaping my world, instead of letting the world shape me.

Gem of Knowledge

When I master inner order, outer chaos loses its power.

82

Reflection 77: I am built to endure storms.

Storms do not break me — they reveal me.

I remind myself: life will bring storms. Unexpected loss, setbacks, betrayals, failures — they will come. But storms are not proof that I am weak. They are the test that proves I was built to endure.

A tree that has stood for decades has faced wind, rain, and fire. And because it endured, it grew deeper roots. I am the same. Every storm I endure drives my roots deeper, makes me more grounded, more unshakable.

Storms hurt. They strip away illusions, they test my patience, they shake my foundation. But when the clouds clear, I remain standing. And every time I endure, I discover that I am stronger than I thought.

I don't pray for a life without storms. I prepare for them. I accept them. I use them. Because storms are where resilience is forged. And I was built for resilience.

Gem of Knowledge

Storms don't break me — they strengthen my roots.

Reflection 78: I push myself where others stop.

Excellence begins at the point where most people quit.

I remind myself: everyone can go until it hurts. Everyone can work until it's tiring. But the difference between ordinary and extraordinary is what happens after that. Most people stop when it's uncomfortable. I push past it.

When my body says "enough," I ask for one more rep. When my mind says "quit," I demand one more step. That's where growth lives — past the line of comfort, past the place where others give in.

I remind myself: the barrier is not real. It's a ceiling built by my own mind. And every time I break through it, I expand who I am. I become someone capable of more than I believed yesterday.

Pushing past the stop is not just about physical effort — it's about mindset. It's about proving that limits are illusions and that persistence is my real strength.

Gem of Knowledge

Where others stop, I begin to grow.

84

Reflection 79: I am calm under pressure.

Pressure doesn't crush me — it sharpens my clarity.

I remind myself: pressure is part of life. Deadlines, challenges, expectations, uncertainty — they all weigh heavy. Most people panic under pressure. They lose focus, they make rash decisions, they collapse. But I refuse to let pressure own me.

When pressure comes, I slow down. I breathe. I remind myself that clarity is my advantage. Panic is noise; calm is strength. Pressure is not here to destroy me — it's here to reveal me.

In the heat of the moment, I don't rush. I don't crack. I choose to remain steady. Because calm under pressure is more powerful than strength in comfort.

I was not built to collapse in the storm. I was built to stand calm, clear, and unshaken until the pressure passes.

Gem of Knowledge

Pressure sharpens me because I remain calm within it.

Reflection 80: I sharpen discipline like a blade.

Discipline grows dull without practice — I sharpen it daily.

I remind myself: discipline is not permanent. It weakens when neglected. It dulls when unused. If I want it sharp, I must sharpen it like a blade.

Sharpening discipline means testing it. It means holding myself accountable when no one is watching. It means saying no to weakness, no to excuses, no to distractions that would soften me.

Each day I train discipline, it cuts cleaner. It allows me to cut through hesitation, through procrastination, through weakness. The sharper my discipline, the easier it becomes to act with clarity and power.

I don't wait for discipline to magically appear. I sharpen it daily, like steel against stone. And because I sharpen it, it never fails me when I need it most.

Gem of Knowledge

The sharper my discipline, the cleaner my victories.

Reflection 81: Each rep, each step, builds the man I become.

Greatness is not built in leaps — it's built in reps.

I remind myself: life is built in the small repetitions. Each rep in the gym, each step in discipline, each act of consistency — they are bricks stacked day by day. Alone they seem small, but together they form the foundation of who I am becoming.

Most people look for a single breakthrough, one big moment that changes everything. But greatness doesn't come from one moment. It comes from thousands of quiet choices, stacked one on top of another.

Every rep is not just for my body — it's for my mind. Every step is not just movement — it's proof that I keep going. These small acts create the man I see in the mirror tomorrow.

So I don't dismiss the little things. I honor them. Because I know they are shaping me more than I can see right now.

Gem of Knowledge

Each rep and each step shape the man I choose to become.

Reflection 82: I turn resistance into strength.

Resistance doesn't block me — it builds me.

I remind myself: resistance shows up in every area of life. It shows up when I want to stay in bed, when I want to avoid the hard work, when I want to quit before I'm finished. Resistance whispers, *"Not today, not now, not you."*

But resistance is not my enemy. It is my training partner. The weight resists me in the gym, yet that very resistance builds my muscle. The same is true for my life. Every moment of resistance is a chance to grow stronger.

Instead of fighting it, I use it. I push into it. I let it sharpen my willpower, deepen my focus, and stretch my endurance. Resistance may make the road harder, but it also makes me tougher. And the more I face it, the more power I build.

Gem of Knowledge

Resistance is the weight that builds my strength.

Reflection 83: My past does not excuse my present.

My past explains me, but it does not excuse me.

I remind myself: I've made mistakes. I've carried pain. I've been shaped by what happened to me. But my past is not a free pass to stay weak today. It may explain where I've been, but it does not excuse where I am going.

I cannot change the past. I cannot erase it. But I can refuse to let it control me. The only thing I control is what I do now. My present choices carry more weight than my past failures.

I remind myself: every day I wake up with a clean slate. I can repeat the story of my past or I can write a new one with my actions today. Excuses tie me down to who I was. Responsibility sets me free to become who I want to be.

Gem of Knowledge

The past is history — the present is my power.

Reflection 84: I am unbreakable when I refuse to quit.

Quitting is the only way to break me.

I remind myself: life will test me. It will hit me with setbacks, failures, and storms. There will be moments I feel shattered, moments I want to collapse. But I know this truth: I cannot be broken if I refuse to quit.

Pain does not break me. Failure does not break me. Pressure does not break me. The only thing that can break me is surrender — and I will not give it.

Every time I keep moving, no matter how small the step, I prove that I am still in the fight. Every time I rise after falling, I prove that I cannot be defeated.

Unbreakable is not about never feeling pain. It's about enduring pain without letting it stop me. It's about choosing persistence over surrender. And as long as I never quit, I remain unbreakable.

Gem of Knowledge

Quitting breaks me; persistence makes me unbreakable.

Reflection 85: I do not run from fear — I walk through it.

Fear loses power when I face it head-on.

I remind myself: fear is natural. It rises before every big step, every risk, every challenge. Most people run from it. But running from fear only makes it bigger.

I choose differently. I don't run from fear — I walk straight through it. I let the fear rise, I acknowledge it, and then I move forward anyway. Fear is not a stop sign. It is a signal that I am on the edge of growth.

Every time I walk through fear, I shrink it. Every time I move despite it, I grow stronger. Fear will always exist, but it will never control me. I may feel it, but I do not obey it.

I remind myself: courage is not the absence of fear — it is the decision to keep walking through it.

Gem of Knowledge

Fear fades when I walk through it.

Reflection 86: I own my choices completely.

My life is not built by luck — it is built by my choices.

I remind myself: I cannot blame the world, the past, or anyone else for where I stand. My life is the result of my choices. Every step I've taken has led me here. And every step I take now will lead me forward.

Owning my choices means I stop making excuses. It means I accept the weight of my decisions and the direction they create. It means I refuse to play the victim.

This is freedom. Because if I created this reality with my choices, then I can create a new one with better choices. Responsibility is not a burden — it is my power.

So I don't hide behind excuses. I own everything I do. Because ownership is strength. Ownership is growth. Ownership is freedom.

Gem of Knowledge

When I own my choices, I own my future.

Reflection 87: I outlast the noise of doubt.

Doubt shouts, but persistence outlasts it.

I remind myself: doubt is loud. It comes from others, from the world, and from within my own mind. It tells me I can't. It tells me I shouldn't. It tells me to stop.

But doubt is temporary. Persistence is permanent. If I keep moving, if I keep showing up, if I keep putting in the work, doubt eventually grows quiet. It cannot outlast me.

I don't waste time arguing with doubt. I don't try to silence it with words. I silence it with results. I silence it by outlasting it, by proving it wrong over and over again with my actions.

Doubt may start the conversation, but persistence always ends it.

Gem of Knowledge

Doubt fades; persistence endures.

Reflection 88: I am patient with the process.

Growth is slow, but slow is not failure.

I remind myself: nothing great is built overnight. Trees take years to grow strong roots. Muscles take months of training to form. Wisdom takes decades of lessons to deepen. Why would my process be any different?

Impatience is the trap. It whispers, *"You should be further by now. It's not working. Stop."* But impatience kills progress. Patience multiplies it.

When I am patient with the process, I stay steady. I don't abandon the work when results don't come fast enough. I keep showing up, keep planting, keep watering, knowing the harvest takes time.

Patience is not passivity — it is discipline. It is me trusting the process, trusting my consistency, trusting that small daily steps add up to something unshakable.

Gem of Knowledge

Patience turns small steps into lasting results.

Reflection 89: I give effort even when no one is watching.

My real character is revealed in the dark, not in the spotlight.

I remind myself: it's easy to perform when eyes are on me, when applause is waiting, when recognition is promised. But what I do in silence, when no one is there to witness, that's who I truly am.

If I only work when I'm seen, I'm weak. But if I give my best when no one is watching, I build unshakable strength. The silent effort, the hidden grind, the unseen hours — these are what make me powerful when the moment of testing comes.

I don't need applause. I don't need validation. My validation comes from knowing I gave everything, whether anyone noticed or not.

Greatness is not built on performance — it's built on character. And my character is built in silence.

Gem of Knowledge

What I do unseen determines who I become in the light.

Reflection 90: I refuse to lie to myself.

The easiest person to fool is myself — and I won't allow it.

I remind myself: self-deception is poison. If I lie to myself — *"I'm doing enough," "I gave my best," "I'll change tomorrow"* — I may comfort myself for a moment, but I rob myself of real growth.

Lies may feel soft, but they harden into weakness. Truth may sting, but it forges strength. I choose truth. Even when it hurts, even when it humbles me, even when it shows me I am not where I want to be.

Facing truth means facing responsibility. It means seeing where I've slacked, where I've made excuses, where I've settled. But in that honesty is the power to change.

I will not lie to myself to stay comfortable. I would rather face the pain of truth and rise than live in the comfort of lies and rot.

Gem of Knowledge

Honesty with myself is the first step to power.

Reflection 91: My self-control is my power.

He who controls himself cannot be controlled.

I remind myself: self-control is not weakness — it is strength in its purest form. Most people are slaves to impulses, to cravings, to emotions. They react to everything. But when I master myself, I become untouchable.

Self-control means I don't give in to every urge. I don't speak every thought. I don't chase every distraction. I choose deliberately, I act with intention, and I move with discipline.

This is my power: to remain steady while others are tossed by their impulses. To remain calm while others lose control. To move with purpose while others scatter.

True strength is not just force — it's restraint. And my self-control makes me stronger than any temptation, stronger than any weakness, stronger than anything outside me.

Gem of Knowledge

My power is measured by my ability to master myself.

Reflection 92: I rise at once when I fall.

The quicker I rise, the less power the fall has.

I remind myself: falling is inevitable. I will stumble, fail, and slip again and again. But the danger is not in the fall — it's in staying down.

When I fall, I rise immediately. I don't wallow. I don't drown in regret. I don't replay the mistake a thousand times. The longer I stay down, the heavier the fall becomes. But the moment I rise, the power returns to me.

Rising quickly is a discipline. It means refusing to let shame or weakness take root. It means standing tall the second I hit the ground and moving forward again.

I don't let the fall define me. I let the rise define me. And the faster I rise, the stronger I become.

Gem of Knowledge

Falling humbles me, rising at once restores me.

Reflection 93: I am a servant to my higher self, not my impulses.

My impulses are loud, but my higher self is wiser.

I remind myself: impulses chase comfort, craving, and quick relief. They want what feels good now, even if it costs me later. My higher self sees beyond the moment. It sees who I am becoming.

I am not here to serve every impulse. I am here to serve the higher version of me — the disciplined me, the purposeful me, the one who chooses strength over weakness.

When impulses rise, I pause. I remind myself: *This is not who I am. This is noise. My higher self decides.* And then I choose what aligns with my vision, not with my craving.

Every time I serve my higher self, I become closer to the person I was meant to be.

Gem of Knowledge

Impulses fade — my higher self endures.

Reflection 94: The harder the road, the stronger I become.

Easy roads don't build me — hard ones do.

I remind myself: the road to strength is not smooth. It is steep, rocky, and full of obstacles. That is by design. The hard road is where character is built, where endurance is forged, where greatness is born.

Every challenge I face, every hardship I endure, every barrier I push through makes me stronger. The harder the road, the more it stretches me, the more it demands of me, the more it shapes me into someone who cannot be broken.

Most people avoid the hard road. They turn back when it gets steep. But I remind myself: this is where the treasure is. This is where the transformation happens. The hard road is my teacher, my builder, my training ground.

I do not fear it. I welcome it. Because every hard road I walk makes me unshakable.

Gem of Knowledge

Hard roads carve me into strength.

Reflection 95: I am my own commander.

I do not wait for orders — I give them.

I remind myself: no one else oversees me. Not my emotions, not my impulses, not the opinions of others. I am the one who decides. I am the one who commands.

A commander does not ask permission. A commander does not beg for motivation. A commander gives clear direction and demands action. That is how I must treat myself. My mind is my army. My body is my soldier. And my spirit is my general.

When doubt rises, I issue the order: *Keep moving.* When fear grows, I issue the order: *Stand tall.* When weakness whispers, I issue the order: *Silence.* I am not a follower of moods or circumstances — I am the commander who sets the path.

This is my authority. This is my power. I lead myself with strength, with clarity, with discipline. And because I do, no one else can control me.

Gem of Knowledge

I am not a follower of impulses — I am the commander of my life.

Reflection 96: My strength is proven daily.

Strength is not a title — it is a practice.

I remind myself: strength is not who I say I am — it is what I prove every day. It is tested in the small choices, in the daily grind, in the moments no one sees.

Every time I rise when I don't feel like it, I prove my strength. Every time I keep moving when I'm tired, I prove my strength. Every time I resist weakness and choose discipline, I prove my strength.

Strength is not built on one grand act. It is proven day by day, moment by moment, choice by choice. And because I keep proving it, it cannot be taken from me.

I don't need to announce it. I don't need to convince anyone. My life shows it. My actions prove it. My consistency speaks for me.

Gem of Knowledge

Strength is proven not once, but daily.

Reflection 97: I can do hard things again and again.

Hard doesn't break me — it builds me.

I remind myself: I've done hard things before. I've faced challenges that felt impossible. I've carried weight I didn't think I could bear. And every time, I rose. Every time, I endured. Every time, I came out stronger.

That's proof. Proof that I can do hard things again. Proof that I can do them not once, but again and again, for as long as it takes.

Hard is not a wall — it is a mirror. It shows me who I really am. And every time I step into hard things, I discover more of my strength, my courage, my discipline.

I don't shy away from the hard. I expect it. I embrace it. I welcome it. Because hard is the forge that keeps shaping me into someone unshakable.

Gem of Knowledge

Hard things are not my limit — they are my training ground.

Reflection 98: I stay steady while others break.

The storm doesn't decide who wins — steadiness does.

I remind myself: life will test everyone. Some will panic. Some will crack. Some will give up. But I remain steady.

Steadiness is not about ignoring the storm — it's about holding my ground in it. While others let fear make their choices, I keep moving with clarity. While others scatter, I stay aligned. While others break, I remain unshaken.

This steadiness is my edge. It means I can outlast pressure, endure chaos, and keep my path clear while others lose theirs. It is not about being perfect — it's about refusing to be moved by fear or weakness.

Because the storm always passes. And when it does, those who broke will be gone. But I'll still be standing.

Gem of Knowledge

My steadiness is my strength when others collapse.

Reflection 99: I out-discipline talent.

Talent shines for a moment — discipline shines forever.

I remind myself: talent is a gift, but it is fragile. It can fade, it can be wasted, it can fail under pressure. Discipline is different. Discipline lasts. Discipline carries me when talent alone cannot.

There are many who are more gifted than me. Smarter. Stronger. Faster. But if they lack discipline, they will not last. And that is where I win.

Discipline outworks talent. Discipline outlasts talent. Discipline turns average into unstoppable. While talent rests, discipline trains. While talent hesitates, discipline acts. While talent fades, discipline rises.

I don't need to be the most talented. I need to be the most disciplined. Because discipline beats talent every time talent refuses to work.

Gem of Knowledge

Talent may open doors — discipline keeps them open.

Reflection 100: My success is earned, not given.

Nothing is owed to me — everything is earned.

I remind myself: success will not be handed to me. No one owes me anything. The world is not waiting to reward me just for existing. If I want it, I must earn it.

Earning success means sacrifice. It means discipline. It means sweat, persistence, and countless hours no one will ever see. It means paying the price when others are unwilling.

When I finally achieve it, I won't look back and say, *"I was lucky."* I'll say, *"I earned this."* And that pride is worth more than any handout.

I don't ask for easy. I don't wait for help. I take full responsibility, because my success is my responsibility.

Gem of Knowledge

What is earned can never be taken away.

Final Reflection: My Discipline Writes My Destiny.

Destiny is not written in stars — it is written in my discipline.

I remind myself: every choice I've made has led me here. Not luck. Not chance. Not fate. My discipline. The days I rose when I didn't want to. The days I pushed when I felt weak. The days I acted without applause, without comfort, without ease. Those days wrote my destiny.

It is not talent that carries me forward. It is not motivation. It is not some hidden gift. It is my discipline. My willingness to show up, to endure, to persist. Discipline has been the ink in which my story is written. And it will be the ink that writes the rest of my future.

I accept that this journey never ends. Discipline does not stop when I reach a goal. Discipline is the foundation for everything that comes next. Every victory, every breakthrough, every transformation begins with the discipline to act again.

So I close this chapter not with finality, but with fire. I will not stop here. I will continue. Because my destiny is not waiting for me — I am creating it. And I create it with discipline, step by step, choice by choice, day by day.

Gem of Knowledge

Discipline is not just my tool — it is the pen that writes my destiny.

Epilogue

The Next Step

You've made it through 100 reflections. A hundred moments of truth, of clarity, of discipline spoken into your life. But this is not the end — it was never meant to be. This is only the beginning.

Mastery is not achieved by reading once. Mastery is built by living these words, daily, relentlessly, without compromise. Each reflection you've read is a tool — but tools are worthless if they remain on the shelf. Pick them up. Use them. Wield them.

You now know the truth: the mind is not your master, it is your servant. Discipline is not your burden, it is your freedom. Strength is not what you are given, it is what you build. And destiny is not written by chance, it is written by your choices.

So what will you do next?
You will repeat. You will return. You will cycle back through these reflections day after day until they become who you are. You will not wait for a sign, you will not wait for permission, you will not wait for the right time. You will move. You will act. You will command.

The world is filled with those who drift, who live at the mercy of moods, of impulses, of weakness. But you are not one of them. You have sharpened your mind. You have claimed your command.

You have chosen discipline over comfort, persistence over excuses, action over passivity.

And now you continue.
Because the last page is not the finish line — it's the call to the next battle, the next test, the next version of you waiting to be forged.

Remember this: your discipline writes your destiny. Not tomorrow. Not someday. Today. In this very moment.

You will stand up. You will take command. You will live the reflections, not just read them. You will step into the life you were meant to build — unshaken, unbroken, and unstoppable.

For the Ones You Love

If this book has sharpened you, don't keep it to yourself. Discipline is not just for you — it's for the ones who walk beside you, the ones who depend on you, the ones you love.

Give this book to someone who needs strength. Someone who needs clarity. Someone who is drifting when they should be rising.

You may not be able to fight their battles, but you can hand them a weapon. And sometimes, that's all it takes to change a life.

Final Words

May your focus be sharp,
your discipline unshakable,
your choices deliberate,
and your destiny written by the strength you
practice daily.

And when the battle of the mind grows loud,
remember the quiet truth within that says:

I believe in me.

The I Believe in Me Gospel Series

The *I Believe in Me Gospel Series* is a collection of books designed to awaken, strengthen, and transform. Each volume delivers direct, powerful truths that cut through illusion, challenge old patterns, and build the inner mastery needed to live fully.

These are not books you simply read — they are practices to live.

100 Reflections to Master Your Mind

www.ingramcontent.com/pod-product-compliance
Lightning Source LLC
Chambersburg PA
CBHW030842090426
42737CB00009B/1068